NATURE HIDE & SEEK

WOODS & FORESTS

John Norris Wood

Illustrated by
Maggie Silver

Alfred A. Knopf, New York

New England woodland:
2 bobcats, 6 woodchucks, 9 eastern chipmunks, 5 opossums, 4 red-tailed hawks, 4 northern copperheads, 3 wood frogs, 8 five-lined skinks, 3 eastern box turtles, 9 katydids. Total: 53 creatures.

Opossum
A mother opossum can carry up to fourteen babies in her pouch. Adult opossums climb trees, using their tails to grip.

Eastern Chipmunk
These striped ground squirrels collect food in huge bulging cheek pouches. Their underground burrow has a bedroom, storeroom, living area, and two entrances.

Bobcat
Although only twice the size of a cat, the bobcat will attack deer and porcupines. It can get close to its prey because it is so well camouflaged.

Katydid
The katydid is a bright green grasshopper with ears on the joints of its front legs. Its wings make the sound "Katy did, she did, she did."

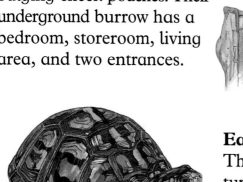

Eastern Box Turtle
The bottom part of this turtle's shell is hinged. It can close the front and back ends together like a box when frightened.

Five-lined Skink

Despite its short legs, this lizard can move very fast. The mother looks after her eggs until they hatch. Only the young have bright blue tails.

Red-tailed Hawk

Year after year this large hawk returns to the same nest to breed. It plays an important part in controlling rodent numbers.

Wood Frog

This frog's colors vary from pink to yellow to brown, but it always has a dark brown stripe by its eyes. Its call is like the quack of a duck.

Northern Copperhead

Copperheads are poisonous and will strike when provoked. They hibernate together in dens through the winter.

Woodchuck

The woodchuck is very inquisitive. When frightened, it whistles and grinds its teeth together. It is very brave and will defend itself fiercely. It hibernates during the coldest weather.

A view from the treetops of a European woodland:
5 tawny owls, 19 fallow deer, 3 wood mice, 2 tree creepers, 3 wrynecks, 3 oak beauty moths, 15 oak beauty caterpillars, 2 buff-tip moths, 8 hunting spiders, 2 pheasants, 3 oak bush crickets. Total: 65 creatures.

Tree Creeper
As it creeps up and down the trunks of trees, this bird probes for insects with its curved bill.

Buff-tip Moth
During the day, this moth rests with its wings wrapped around its body, looking like a broken twig.

Common Pheasant
The hen pheasant is marked by her brown, patterned feathers, and the male is brilliantly colored. They are bred as "game" birds to be hunted.

Hunting Spider
This green spider sits hidden in the leaves catching unsuspecting insects.

Wood Mouse
The wood mouse mainly comes out at night looking for insects, nuts, and berries to eat. It stores nuts in its nest for the winter.

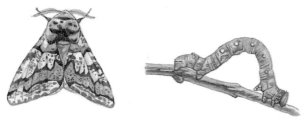

Tawny Owl

The tawny owl calls "hoo, hoo, hoo, hooo," but when searching for mice with its huge eyes, the design of its special feathers enables it to fly silently and swoop down without warning.

Oak Beauty Moth and Caterpillar

Both the moth and its caterpillar are well disguised among the trees.

Fallow Deer

The patterns on the deer's coat help to hide it in the forest. In winter, it changes to gray to match the bare trees. The males have antlers, which they shed and grow again in spring.

Wryneck

This rare member of the woodpecker family twists its head at odd angles, hence its name.

Oak Bush Cricket

The male cricket calls to the female by drumming its back feet on leaves.

European woodland floor:
2 woodcocks, 6 hedgehogs, 3 bank voles, 3 common frogs, 2 smooth newts,
2 stag beetles, 8 common garden snails, 6 pill wood lice, 3 nut weevils,
17 wood ants. Total: 52 creatures.

Wood Ant

Several thousand wood ants live in one large nest made of leaves and twigs. They collect food in their jaws and carry it back to their home.

Common Frog

The frog searches for small insects, which it catches by suddenly shooting out its sticky tongue.

Common Garden Snail

On damp nights, snails move from their resting places to look for plants to eat.

Hedgehog

Hedgehogs sleep by day, and look for insects, slugs, and snails to eat at night. Newly born hedgehogs have only a few soft prickles, which later harden.

Stag Beetle

The jaws of the male stag beetle look like miniature antlers. These beetles are good fliers. Their larvae feed on dead wood.

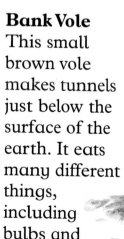

Pill Wood Louse

If you disturb a pill wood louse, it rolls into a perfect ball or "pill."

Woodcock

During the day, the woodcock stays hidden. At dusk, it prods the earth for worms with its long bill. If her chicks are in danger, the mother will fly them to safety in her claws.

Nut Weevil

This insect's nose is like a stiff version of an elephant's trunk. It gnaws holes in hazelnuts and lays an egg in each one.

Bank Vole

This small brown vole makes tunnels just below the surface of the earth. It eats many different things, including bulbs and insects.

Smooth Newt

Unlike lizards, newts have no scales. They live in water and on land, where they feed on slugs and earthworms.

Northern European Pine forest:
2 brown bears, 8 wild boars, 6 foxes, 7 badgers, 2 pine martens, 20 rabbits,
4 moles, 2 nightjars, 4 pine hawk moths. Total: 55 creatures.

Pine Hawk moth

At night, this moth
flits between flowers,
sipping nectar with
its long tongue. Its
caterpillars feed
on pine needles.

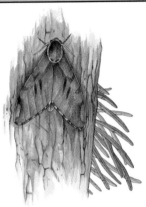

Badger

Although badgers
and foxes sometimes live in
burrows that connect, they never
mix. They tunnel deep into the
ground, making a series of
chambers called a sett. Badgers
eat insects, fruit, and mice.

Wild Boar

The huge canine teeth of this
fierce and rare animal are
razor-sharp, and boars will
eat almost anything.
Young piglets are camouflaged
by their stripes.

Rabbit

Until they move, showing their white tails,
rabbits are difficult to see. They live in warrens,
and the bucks thump their feet on the ground
to warn of approaching danger.

Pine Marten
The beautiful pine marten is so agile that it can catch squirrels and even birds in the treetops.

Brown Bear
At night, brown bears search for honey, vegetables, and small animals, although their eyesight is poor. They live alone in dens and are protected from hunters by law.

Fox
Foxes hunt for rabbits, insects, birds, and even garbage in towns. They are very clever and can run long distances. When hunted, they may swim through water to disguise their strong scent.

Mole
Moles must eat more than their own weight in earthworms every day or they die. They are designed for life underground with large front paws for digging and tiny eyes.

Nightjar
This perfectly camouflaged bird feeds in midair by catching night-flying insects in its wide mouth.

European Deciduous woodland:
2 common toads, 2 gray squirrels, 4 wrens, 3 common dormice, 3 pygmy shrews, 4 green hairstreak butterflies, 3 peppered moths, 9 peppered moth caterpillars, 3 parent bugs, 2 wood crickets, 7 lacewings, 7 smooth-coiled snails.
Total: 49 creatures.

Smooth-coiled Snail

These tiny snails are found in large numbers on tree trunks and hiding under woodland debris.

Wren

These small birds have a surprisingly loud song. In winter, they huddle together for warmth.

Green Hairstreak Butterfly

This butterfly, with green, leaf-like underwings guards its territory and drives off other insects with little skirmishing flights.

Common Toad

The toad feeds on insects. It is well camouflaged and tastes nasty to other animals. It can live for twenty years. Every so often it pulls off its old skin and swallows it as it grows a new skin.

Pygmy Shrew

The pygmy shrew is tiny, about the size of this picture. It lives for less than a year, and must eat its body weight in insects every day.